lonely planet

NOT-FOR-PARENTS

U.S.A.
Everything you ever
wanted
to know

Lynette Evans

CONTENTS

I'M FEELING A BIT LIGHTHEADED.

I WONDER WHO'LL BE TAKING ME HOME TONIGHT.

DO MY SHOULDERS LOOK BIG IN THIS?

WHO ARE YOU CALLING A CLOWN?

NOT-FOR-PARENTS

THIS IS NOT A GUIDEBOOK. And it is definitely Not-for-parents.

IT IS THE REAL, INSIDE STORY about one of the world's most exciting countries—the United States of America. In this book you'll hear fascinating tales about the Wild West, **cockroach races**, a massive canyon, and weddings in Vegas.

Check out cool stories about **candy bars** and movie stars, beauty queens and **blue jeans**. You'll find astronauts, **gangsters**, pilgrims, and some amazingly **heroic dogs**.

This book shows you a **UNITED STATES** your parents probably don't even know about.

GREAT STATES

In Utah, birds have the right of way on highways. In Kansas, restaurants were once not allowed to serve cherry pie with ice cream on Sundays. And in Texas, there is a town called Ding Dong! There are 50 states in the USA, and each has its own weird and wonderful ways.

Alaska

Staggering stats
Alaska is the biggest state. It's more than three times the size of France!

I THINK I CAN SEE HAWAII.

State symbols
States often have official birds, flowers, and songs. Arizona even has an official state fossil— no, it's not your grandma, it's petrified wood!

Pacific Ocean

Hawaii

Something fishy
Hawaii is the only island state. It has a tiny state fish with a monstrous name: humuhumunukunukuapua'a—it's a real mouthful!

Four corners
Thomas Jefferson wasn't a square, but he did suggest the western states be divided into a geometric pattern. At Four Corners, you can be in Utah, Colorado, Arizona, and New Mexico at the same time.

The first 13
The United States grew out of 13 original colonies.
Can you figure out their abbreviations? MA, NH, NY,
RI, CT, NJ, DE, PA, MD, VA, NC, SC, GA.

Name game
Massachusetts has been nicknamed
the "Baked Bean State," Montana the
"Stub Toe State," and Missouri the
"Puke State," although no one knows
why that name was brought up!

MY ARM'S GETTING SORE.

Atlantic Ocean

State of indecision
The District of Columbia
(Washington, DC) is the
capital city. Some people
argue that DC should be
the 51st state.

RE WE ERE YET?

Gulf of Mexico

WANT MORE?

Maine is the only one-syllable state ☆ www.50states.com/facts

MADE IN THE USA

Benjamin Franklin was born in Boston, Massachusetts on January 17, 1706. He was bafflingly brilliant in everything he turned his hand to, and an expert in matters ranging from how to grow cabbages to how to avoid flatulence, and how to shape the Declaration of Independence. He was an author, a diplomat, a scientist, and an inventor of many useful objects.

Busy Ben
The days weren't long enough for all of Ben's busy schemes. He set up a postal system, a fire department, America's first city hospital, and its first circulating library. He also proposed Daylight Saving Time. Wasn't that brilliant!

FRANKLIN'S FIRSTS

One of America's most frantic inventors, Benjamin Franklin had so many bright ideas he must have dazzled himself!

☆ bifocals—to avoid having to switch between glasses for distance and glasses for reading

☆ lightning rod—to protect buildings from lightning strikes and resulting fires

☆ grabber, or longarm—an extendable device for taking things off high shelves

☆ Franklin stove—emitted more heat and used less fuel to heat homes

☆ writing chair—a desk and chair in one

☆ swim fins—wooden flippers for hands and feet for faster swimming

☆ odometer—a device to measure the distance a vehicle travels

PEOPLE ARE REALLY BRIGHT AROUND HERE!

Ben Franklin didn't want to patent or profit from any of his inventions.

NOW I UNDERSTAND ELECTRICITY. IT'S HIT ME LIKE A BOLT OF LIGHTNING!

WORLD-CHANGERS

Wired for sound

Alexander Graham Bell—okay, he was born in Scotland—got a US patent for his telephone in 1876. The new-fangled device was so startling that many people picked up the receiver and just listened.

Electrifying experiments

Some of Ben's early experiments with electricity were real knockouts. He tried to zap a turkey with an electric shock once, but stunned himself instead!

Lighting the way

Thomas Alva Edison had a hoard of inventions, but electric lighting was the most brilliant of them all. City officials in Florida were a bit dim when they turned down his offer to light the streets at night, though. They thought cows would be kept awake by Edison's bright lights!

Musical moments

Ben even invented an instrument that spun glass bowls on a rod, and made music when touched with wet fingers! Mozart and Beethoven were so impressed by his "glass armonica" that they composed music for it!

Keeping connected

Facebook was founded by Mark Zuckerberg from his Harvard dorm in 2004. He originally named it "Facemash." You want gravy with that?

WANT MORE?

Ben the inventor ☆ www.fi.edu/franklin/inventor

BATTLE OF THE GREASY GRASS

His name was Sitting Bull, but he didn't take the injustices of life sitting down! The famous medicine man inspired the Sioux and other tribes of the Great Plains to unite and fight to save their lands, and defend their way of life. In 1876, Native American forces wiped out US Army leader George Custer and 267 of his men in less than an hour. Many know the famous fight as the Battle of the Little Bighorn, but to the Sioux it is the Battle of the Greasy Grass.

Sparks fly
The Great Sioux War began in 1874 when Custer led an expedition into the sacred Sioux land of the Black Hills near Montana seeking gold.

WHAT IS IT WITH ALL THIS "SITTING" AND "STANDING" ANYWAY?

Jumping Badger to Sitting Bull
Jumping Badger was born in about 1831 in South Dakota. As a boy, he did everything slowly and carefully. His father gave him the name Sitting Bull after he showed bravery in a battle.

George Custer

Custer died in the battle, which is also known as "Custer's Last Stand."

Super-power shirt

When preparing to fight an enemy armed with guns, a shirt that repelled bullets would be the gear to wear! Sioux warriors performed a ritual called the Ghost Dance. They believed the shirt they wore in the dance would deflect bullets.

At least 2,000 Sioux and Cheyenne warriors joined forces in the battle.

HORSE POWER

Christopher Columbus made a big impact when he stumbled upon the Americas in the 1490s. He called the native people *Indios*, which became "Indians," and on his second voyage he brought a new kind of animal to America—the horse! Before long, Cheyenne, Comanche, and Apache were hunting across the Great Plains on horseback. Sioux first traded for horses around 1730 and quickly became super-skilled horseback warriors.

OUCH, I WISH COLUMBUS HAD BROUGHT SADDLES, TOO!

Hunger games

During the fighting between the Sioux and the US Army in the 1800s, the army slaughtered vast numbers of bison to try to starve the Sioux and make them give up.

WANT MORE?

PUBLIC ENEMY #1?

His business card said that he was a "Used Furniture Dealer," but America's most wanted gangster was the king of dirty dealings and shady underworld crime. Despite his dark side, he dressed in cheerful suits, wore a squeaky-clean white felt hat, and flashed a dazzling 11.5-carat diamond ring on his pinky finger! "Big Al" was a big mob boss, but was he a murderous monster through and through?

AL CAPONE
OFFICIAL NAME: ALPHONSE GABRIEL "AL" CAPONE

ALIAS: SCARFACE (DUE TO A RAZOR CUT TO HIS CHEEK IN A FIGHT)

BORN: JANUARY 17, 1899 IN BROOKLYN, NYC

DIED: JANUARY 25, 1947

CAUSE OF DEATH: HEALTH COMPLICATIONS

Souped up or cleaned up?

To some, Al Capone was a Robin Hood figure who fought for the rights of the working people. At the onset of the Great Depression in 1929, he opened the nation's first soup kitchen for the needy. It served three free meals a day *and* helped clean up Al's image.

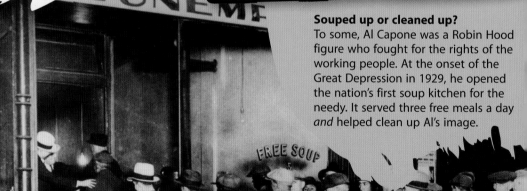

MILK MOBSTERS

Al Capone usually dealt in bottles of illegal, bootlegged alcohol, but he and his brother Ralph "Bottles" Capone also ran a milk distributing company. During the Great Depression, Capone donated millions of bottles of milk to schoolchildren and "Bottles" fought to make it a law that the sell-by date was stamped on so the children weren't given sour milk to drink.

The law finally managed to nail Al Capone for evading taxes.

Murder and massacre

It should be a day of love hearts, but February 14, 1929 was a day of bleeding hearts when a massacre took place in Chicago. With Capone as most likely mastermind, the hit involved members of his family masquerading as policemen to destroy a rival Chicago gang.

I'VE ALWAYS WANTED TO BE A BIG HIT!

Public enemies list

The *Chicago Tribune* newspaper published a "Public Enemies" list on April 24, 1930. Al Capone was number 1 on the list. His brother Ralph was number 2. Bet their parents were proud... NOT!

A prison cell at Alcatraz

HERE COMES NUMBER 1!

WANT MORE?

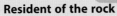

Resident of the rock

Capone ruled the roost even when behind bars. When he had his prison cell in Atlanta carpeted and a radio to entertain visitors installed, he was shipped off to the rugged and remote Alcatraz Island for a rockier jailbird experience. Is that why it's called AL-catraz?

Get the inside story on gangsters and racketeers ☆ themobmuseum.org

ALL-AMERICAN ACCIDENTS

Pop, fizz, aahhh! Happiness is when an accidental invention turns out to be what everyone is gasping for! In 1886, a pharmacist named John Pemberton brewed up a murky mix of ingredients to make a remedy for headaches. He carried a jug of his syrupy concoction to a pharmacy in downtown Atlanta, where they added a dash of seltzer, declared it delicious, and sold it for five cents a glass. Coca-Cola has made a real splash ever since!

When POP goes BANG

Walter E. Diemer was an accountant at a chewing gum factory, but one day he didn't stick to his task. He experimented with gum recipes instead and made a batch of not-too-sticky, stretchy goop. Blowing bubbles became totally POPular!

BITE ME!

Cookie time

In 1930, an innkeeper named Ruth Wakefield ran out of baking chocolate while making cookies. So she chopped up a chocolate bar and added it to the dough, expecting the chunks to melt. They didn't, and her gooey chocolate chip cookies have been munched and crunched ever since.

Waffling around

Ice creams were such a hot item at the St. Louis World's Fair in 1904 that the seller ran out of dishes. Quick as a lick, a nearby pastry maker rolled his waffles into a cone shape to hold the treat. He was no drip, was he?

POPSICLE PARADISE

In 1905, eleven-year-old Frank Epperson was making soda pop, but he left his mixing bucket out overnight and the drink froze with the wooden stick standing up. Did forgetful Frankie get a licking? No. He sold his amazing icicles!

WANT MORE?

Make your own ice pops! ☆ kids-cooking-activities.com/Popsicle-recipes.html

BLUE JEAN SCENE

Do you ever think you look as big as a tent or as wide as a wagon in your blue jeans? It may be because the first work pants made by Levi Strauss during the rough and tumble gold-mining days were fashioned from a heavy-duty canvas fabric meant for tents and wagon covers! When the miners moaned that their pants were falling apart, Levi came to the rescue with sturdy denim overalls and copper rivets. Levi's were born in the United States, and they've stood the test of time.

> LEVI STRAUSS WAS A TOTAL JEAN-IUS!

Riveting stuff
The name "denim" comes from the French fabric Levi used to make the miners' pants—"serge de Nimes." Sailors from the Italian town of Genoa wore pants made of this denim—that's why the pants are called "jeans."

> I COME FROM A LONG LINE OF MINERS. MUST BE IN THE JEANS!

Smarty-pants
Levi Strauss never wore a pair of jeans in his life! He manufactured them as overalls for laborers, and he was a well-heeled businessman. But Levi always made sure the workwear was top quality.

Teens in jeans

Thanks to movie star James Dean (or is it Dames Jean?), jeans became a symbol of freedom and rebellious youth during the 1950s. Teens in jeans were banned from restaurants, cinemas, and even school!

I'M A REBEL WITHOUT A CAUSE.

BEHIND THE SEAMS

☆ Each year, 2 billion pairs of jeans are sold worldwide, around 780 million in the United States alone.

☆ May 20 is the birthday of jeans. On this day in 1873, Levi Strauss and Jacob Davis patent their riveted denim pants in the United States.

☆ US soldiers introduce jeans to the rest of the world during World War II. They wear them off-duty, of course!

☆ A Japanese buyer pays $60,000 for a pair of 115-year-old Levi's 501 jeans in 2005.

☆ Dussault Apparel's Trashed Denim jeans are the most expensive. They are decorated with rubies, diamonds, and gold and cost a cool $250,000!

WANT MORE?

Visit Levi's HQ ☆ **www.levistrauss.com**

SPACED OUT

Space fever gripped America during the 1960s, but the nation wasn't just aiming for the stars—it was shooting for the Moon. In 1969, the National Aeronautics and Space Administration (NASA) successfully landed the first men on the moon. Since then, it has launched rockets, satellites, shuttles, and astronauts into space. It has put rovers on Mars and scientists on the International Space Station, but what's it like living in zero gravity?

Liquid cooling garment

Control module

That's potty!
Without gravity, using a toilet can be tricky. When the space shuttle *Endeavour* launched in 1993, it carried a new toilet system with an out-of this-world price tag. It cost $23.4 million for the high-tech space toilet, which contained 4,000 parts, including foot holds and thigh bars to keep an astronaut safely anchored!

Darn cool diapers
Astronauts couldn't survive for more than a few seconds in space without a spacesuit. These outfits are not to be whipped off when nature calls, however. Instead, diapers, or maximum absorbency garments, in the suit allow an astronaut to "go" on the go!

U.S.
★ First To Moon ★

ARMSTRONG–COLLINS–ALDRIN
JULY 20th 1969
APOLLO 11

OVER THE MOON

On July 20, 1969, two *Apollo 11* astronauts, Neil Armstrong and Buzz Aldrin, became the first people to walk on the Moon. The mission's third astronaut, Michael Collins, orbited in the Command Module ready to fly his Moonwalking buddies home to a hero's welcome.

Food to go
In space, food and drink can easily escape. Even the smell of food can float away, so an astronaut's appetite is often lessened.

Absorption garment

Vomit comet
Astronauts train to get used to the feeling of weightlessness in space and most suffer from space sickness. Floating vomit is a nasty hazard during a mission. Luckily, "barf bags" and suction devices can capture it!

WANT MORE?

EXPRESS DELIVERY

If you are skinny, breathtakingly brave, and able to ride a horse at breakneck speed, you may have had the right stuff to deliver mail during the days of the perilous Pony Express. If you can laugh in the face of danger—and happen to be an orphan—you'd have the job in the bag for sure! In 1860, daring Pony Express riders thundered across treacherous trails from Missouri to California, riding rough day and night, rain or shine, to make sure the mail went through.

Speed read
It usually took ten days for riders to race the Pony Express route. But the mail sailed through at record speed when President Lincoln's Inaugural Address was delivered in 7 days, 13 hours. Those were some pooped ponies

WANTED

YOUNG, SKINNY, WIRY FELLOWS

NOT OVER EIGHTEEN. MUST BE EXPERT RIDERS, WILLING TO RISK DEATH DAILY.

ORPHANS PREFERRED. WAGES $25 PER WEEK.

APPLY, PONY EXPRESS STABLE, St. Joseph, Missouri

Delivery boy
Legend has it that the youngest rider of the Pony Express was a lad named "Bronco Charlie" Miller. He was just eleven when he hit the mail trail.

I heard it straight from the horse's mouth: mail to San Francisco in just ten days!

I WONDER IF THEY SERVE "EXPRESS"-O ON THE PONY EXPRESS—I THINK I NEED ONE!

A letter bringing news of Lincoln's election, delivered by Pony Express.

Getting licked

The Pony Express was a fast and furious operation. The horseback relay mail service took off on April 3, 1860, but it came to a halt on October 24, 1861 when the nation got wired with telegraph technology.

WANT MORE?

AMERICA'S MAIN STREET

Running more than halfway across the United States, Route 66 was one of America's first paved highways. Stretching for almost 2,485mi (4,000km), this famous road weaves west from Chicago, through the heart of America, and ends in LA where Pacific breakers pound the pier. It is home to muscle cars, Harleys, hitchhikers, and road-trippers.

Route 66 is called the "Mother Road," the "Glory Road," and "America's Main Street."

A SMASH HIT

Route 66 was a mecca for motorists when it opened in 1926. It connected small towns with large cities and became a hot spot for mom-and-pop cafés, larger-than-life advertising, and unique motels.

Sign of the times
Before the highway was officially decommissioned in 1985, the Route 66 road marker was one of the most commonly stolen signs

California

Greetings from LOS ANGELES CALIFORNIA

Arizona

New Mexico

Texas

It's Mr. Big to you
Route 66 is also known as a "highway of icons." Super-sized statues stand in front of many shops and roadside restaurants to lure customers.

Route 66 music and lyrics ☆ www.lyricsdepot.com/nat-king-cole/route-66.html

CRAZY CONTESTS

People go all out in the United States,
and when it comes to the many wild and wacky contests
across the country, competitors don't dis their rivals—even
if they're bugs! Cockroach racing is a long-standing US
tradition. Roaches even get involved in choosing
the president. Gentlemen, start your insects!

Tearing up the track
Indiana is famous for racing,
but who would've thought
hissing cockroaches would be
tearing around tracks! At the
BugBowl, ripped roaches race
with tiny tractors, which
must be a real drag!

Cow chip chucking
The town of Beaver in Oklahoma proudly
claims the title of "Cow Chip Throwing
Capital of the World!" Each April,
contestants show off their dung-flinging
skills. A bad chip can really get you in the
poop, though—it pays to take time to
find the perfect projectile for a solid start

UTTER HOGWASH

YOU'RE ON THE HAM, I MEAN HOME, STRETCH NOW!

Panting pigs

At the Kansas State Fair, there's no time for little piggies to get porky! The annual Pig Races draw plenty of cheering crowds as the hogs hightail it around the race track—whoever said that pigs don't fly?

HERE PIGGY, PIGGY, PIGGY!

Hog hollerin'

With bonafide judges and real rules, hog-calling contests have created a ruckus at state picnics and fairs since early days—and there's more to the sport than being able to squeal like a stuck pig. Contestants must mimic the calls made by hogs, and they are judged on how loudly and clearly they can shriek "SOOO-EY" to the fine swine!

issin' in high places

ssing cockroaches often head to head in election ears to predict the outcome f the US presidential race. lthough roach races have orrectly predicted White ouse winners 80% f the time, it bugs people hen they get it wrong!

Roach fans

In 1933, at the Nut Club in New York, fans cheer as cockroaches race for the finish line!

WANT MORE?

Compete in a "Rolling in Grits" competition! ☆ www.worldgritsfestival.com

PRESIDENTIAL PETS

It's very white, very grand, and very famous, but it's also a place that the US president and family can call home. And what's a home without pets frolicking on the lush lawns? Cats, dogs, and ponies have been popular pets at the White House—but not all the animals that take up residence at this presidential pad are so predictable!

THIS SPEECH WILL REALLY KNOCK THEIR SOCKS OFF!

Sock it to 'em!

The Clintons had a cat named Socks. This famous first feline even answered fan mail on White House stationery and had his own phone line to field calls from fans. Socks rocks

DON'T DROP THE BALL, MR. PRESIDENT!

First Dog

Not everyone needs to be voted into the White House. Bo the Portuguese water dog was a gift to President Barack Obama's family from a senator. His favorite food is tomatoes and his hobbies include playing on the White House lawn. It's a dog's life!

Bo during a white-out at the White House

PARADE OF FIRST PETS

☆ No doggy breath for President George Washington! His American staghound was named Sweet Lips.

☆ Thomas Jefferson had a mockingbird that was trained to eat food out of his mouth!

☆ Theodore Roosevelt practically had a zoo. His pets included a zebra, hyena, coyote, and a one-legged rooster! (Was that thanks to the coyote?)

The wackiest White House pet was a pygmy hippo owned by President Coolidge!

President Kennedy with Macaroni the pony

THE KIDS WILL EAT THEIR PASTA FASTER WITH ME AROUND!

President Johnson's beagles, Him and Her

Paws and jaws

President Hoover had a dog named King Tut that patrolled the White House grounds. Hoover also had two crocodiles. Hope they didn't make him snap!

I'VE TAUGHT HIM TO SHAKE PAWS.

WANT MORE?

Presidents and their pets ☆ www.presidentialpetmuseum.com

MR. HOT POTATO

Have you ever been told not to play with your food? When it comes to spuds, rules go right out the window, and the fun and games begin. In 1952, an inventor named George Lerner made a silly set of push-pin plastic pieces for poking into any piece of produce around. He named his funny-face toy Mr. Potato Head, and it is a piping-hot seller to this day. The googly-eyed spud is even a TV and blockbuster movie star although, with his quick-change acts, he is no couch potato!

National spokespud
Mr. Potato Head used to smoke a pipe, but in 1987, he cleaned up his act and became an ambassador—or spokespud—for the American Cancer Society's Great American Smokeout Campaign. His little plastic pipe went up in smoke!

Mr. and Mrs. Potato Head lead a star-studded cast of toys in the Disney/Pixar blockbuster, Toy Story.

Rotten potatoes
A Mr. Potato Head toy came only with parts at the start—buyers had to supply a pokable potato. He got a body after parents kept finding rotten potatoes growing eyes of their own beneath children's beds!

YOU ARE THE APPLE OF MY EYE—OR IS IT POTATO?

Potato parade
Mr. Potato Head is a regular at the Macy's Thanksgiving Day Parade. Probably giving thanks he's not the main course for Thanksgiving dinner.

I've got eyes for you
Mr. Potato Head was a real stud for a spud! In 1953, he got all mushy over a girl potato and Mrs. Potato Head hit the scene. The two couldn't take their eyes off each other!

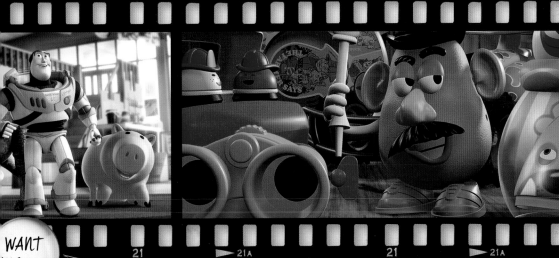

WANT MORE?

Toy Hall of Fame ☆ www.toyhalloffame.org/toys

FIRST FAMILIES

Imagine waving goodbye to everything you know. At least 30 children stood bravely at the rail of the *Mayflower* as it set sail from England to America in 1620. Nine-year-old Love Brewster and her little brother Wrestling were among them. They would have been excited at first, but after being tossed about on heaving seas for 65 days in cramped conditions, land would have been a happy sight—even just a little rock might do!

Mayflower

> MY EYEBROWS NEED A TRIM—I CAN BARELY SEE!

> DRAT, MY SHOELACE IS UNDONE!

A game of knickers?
With 102 passengers, there wasn't much space for fun and games aboard the *Mayflower*. Once they had landed, Pilgrim children built forts and climbed trees. They played a game of marbles known as "knickers," but only after they had finished their chores!

Newfound friends
The Pilgrims struggled to grow crops in their new homeland. But help arrived when two Native Americans— Samoset and Squanto—taught the Pilgrims how to hunt, fish, and grow crops, such as squash and corn.

Two children were born onboard! A baby named Oceanus Hopkins was born at sea. Little Peregrine White was born when the ship anchored.

THE FIRST THANKSGIVING

Thanks to friendships with the Wampanoag tribe, the Pilgrims had a bumper harvest by the fall of 1621. They invited the Wampanoag to share in a Thanksgiving feast—and started a tradition.

> HOPE THERE'S NO LEEKS ON THE MENU, WE HAD ENOUGH OF THOSE ON THE MAYFLOWER!

> MAMA, MY LEGS FEEL LIKE JELLY. AND SO DO I!

> IT SEEMED LIKE A GOOD IDEA AT THE TIME!

The black sheep of Plymouth
One Pilgrim family, the Billingtons, were real troublemakers. Son Francis fired a musket in the cabin of the *Mayflower*. Another son, John Jr., went missing and was eventually returned by natives. Mom Eleanor was whipped for slander. And dad, John Sr., was hanged for murder!

WANT MORE?

All the children survived the journey on the *Mayflower* ☆ www.mayflowerhistory.com

GRAND ADVENTURE

The Grand Canyon delivers adventure on a grand scale. Everything about this super-sized, seriously spectacular hole in the ground is grand, from the rocky rim with its dizzying views, to plunging cliff walls, and monster rapids on a river that bucks like a bronco on steroids! No wonder it is one of the seven natural wonders of the world.

A Major mission

In 1869, Civil War amputee John Wesley Powell was the first white guy to lead an expedition on the Colorado River through the Grand Canyon. It was a white-knuckle ride on white-water rapids. Sounds mad, but he was definitely arm-less!

AAAHHH, RIDING THE RAPIDS IS SUCH A RUSH!

Skywalk talk
Even Buzz Lightyear would get dizzy at this height! A glass skywalk 4,000ft (1,220m) above the canyon floor delivers vertigo on a large scale.

CANYON CRITTERS

The rocky canyons are home to wildlife such as deer, pumas, coyotes, squirrels, rattlers, and big horn sheep.

I'M NOT A MULE, DEAR. I'M A MULE DEER!

The Grand Canyon, in Arizona, is **277mi (446km)** long and plummets to a depth of about **1mi (1.6km).**

DON'T PUSH ME. I'M A SQUIRREL ON THE EDGE!

About 5 million visitors view the Grand Canyon each year. Many get wet!

THIS WILL BE ONE GREAT LEAP FOR A SHEEP!

WANT MORE?

CLOSE ENCOUNTERS

Most critters steer clear of pesky humans, but some are bold enough to risk close encounters. Bears will venture into cars, tents, and backyards in search of a snack. They may look cute and cuddly but these real-life teddies can cause mischief and mayhem!

Grizzly end
John "Grizzly" Adams captured and trained bears for zoos and circuses. During his life he was attacked by bears and tigers, but he died in 1860 after being bitten by a monkey!

HE'S "GRIZZLY" AND I'M "BENJAMIN?" THAT'S ODD.

Most grizzly bear attacks are by females defending their cubs. Black bear attacks are usually by hungry males!

Grizzly Adams named his favorite bear Benjamin Franklin.

Bear with a sore head
When one apple-snitching bear was disturbed in the backyard by a pet dog, things turned ugly. The pooch owner had to pluck a giant squash from the garden and bop the bear on the head until it backed off.

...ast food?
...hen one nosy bear sniffed ...peanut-butter sandwich ...side a car, he climbed in ...nd accidentally hit the gear ...tick. The car rolled downhill, ...iving the bear such a scare ...hat he pooped on the seat!

A bear can smell a carcass from as far away as 20mi (32km)!

I CAN SMELL YOU WATCHING ME.

FOOD
TORAGE
EQUIRED

THE BEAR FACTS

★ Grizzly bears feast on salmon, hunt moose, and also eat insects.

★ Black bears are not always black. They can be brown, white, blue-black, or black.

★ Polar bears don't have white fur. They have black skin and see-through hairs to trap heat.

★ Bears are thought to have a keener sense of smell than any other animal on the planet. They can smell 2,100 times better than a human can.

Polar bear

WANT MORE?

Stay safe in bear country ★ www.nps.gov/grsm/naturescience/black-bears.htm

GOLD RUSH

Sometimes, something that glitters IS gold! In 1848, workers at a sawmill in California found shiny rocks that turned out to be gold nuggets. Word spread like wildfire and prospectors rode on mules, in wagons, or aboard vomit-making ships to reach the rich goldfields of California. No matter how the fortune-seekers traveled, however, rushing for gold was slow going.

Dirty work
The few women that joined the gold rush often made a fortune dealing in dirty laundry. In fact, many miners found it cheaper to ship their shirts to Hawaii for cleaning!

IT SHINES, SHIMMERS, GLITTERS, AND GLEAMS. I HOPE I HAVEN'T CAUGHT ANOTHER LITTLE FISHIE!

CALIFORNIA GOLD RUSH 1849

USA 33

Forty-niners
The first gold nuggets were found by James Marshall on January 24, 1848 at Sutter's Mill, California. The discovery sparked a rush to the region. The miners were called "Forty-Niners"— it took them a while to get there!

> WHAT'S THE RUSH? PLENTY OF GOLD HERE.

Hangtown fry

In Hangtown, gold-snitchers and lawbreakers were hanged. It wasn't all doom though. One newly rich miner strolled into a restaurant and ordered the most expensive dish the cook could whip up. People called his fancy fry-up of eggs, bacon, and oysters "Hangtown Fry."

> I'M NO FOOL. THIS HERE'S REAL GOLD!

GOLD FEVER

About 80,000 gold-seekers poured into California from all over the world in 1849. Many dug from dawn till dusk to strike it rich. In 1852 prospectors bagged around $81 million worth of gold. But by the late 1850s, the gold was all panned out.

WANT MORE?

Many gold-diggers came from China. They called California the "Gold Mountain."

TORNADO ALLEY

There are many ups and downs in real estate, but nothing as shattering as having your house picked up by a monster storm that spins it around, then drops it down the street! The twisters that tear through Tornado Alley are often deadly. Knowing they'll face an arsenal of torrential rain, relentless hail, and gale-force winds, most people take shelter from the fury, but not storm chasers. That's when these mad scientists whirl in to work!

IS THAT A FLYING SNAKE, FOR GOODNESS SAKE?

Prime tornado time: March through August, afternoon to evening.

MEAN AND EXTREME

About 1,000 tornadoes hit the United States every year, and most strike the central states of Oklahoma, Kansas, the Texas Panhandle, Nebraska, South Dakota, and Colorado. Tornadoes will sometimes lift and destroy houses, but leave light objects like paper and plates undisturbed. They have been known to toss trains, suck up snakes, and even pluck the feathers from chickens!

This mattress sprung out of bed when the storm struck.

Sucked up
During a tornado in Kansas, a woman took cover in her bathroom. She grabbed hold of the toilet, but was then sucked up by the twister and knocked out by flying debris (which hopefully did not come from the toilet)! She was rescued by two superhero storm chasers.

> HOLY COW. THIS IS NOT THE BEST WAY TO MAKE A MILKSHAKE!

TWIRLING TWISTERS

Tornadoes are born inside a big thunderstorm and created by powerful, twisting winds that form a freaky looking funnel. From the outside, tornadoes can look like snaking ropes, cones, or elephant trunks. Debris clouds show that a tornado has reached the ground.

> WHAT IS THIS, THE TORNADO TANGO?

Twist and shout
You might think storm chasers are adrenaline junkies, but most are scientists who study how supercell storms form. They use heavy-duty equipment to gather data in deadly conditions.

Average tornado alert warning time: 13 minutes.

WANT MORE?

Meet the Cyclone Cowboy ☆ www.stormchaser.com

CHOW DOWN

They'll slap a sizzling-hot meat patty between two buns, with all the mouthwatering fixings—pickles, oozy ketchup and mustard, melted cheese, and perhaps some super-sloppy chili on top. There it is, the glorious burger, giant of the fast-food world. And with an order of piping-hot fries on the side and a shake to wash it all down, you've got it made. Fast, easy, cheap food to go is simply as American as apple pie!

FACE-STUFFING

According to Major League Eating, stuffing your face with as much food as you can within a set time is actually a sport! Participants in competitive eating contests are likely to end up with more than just egg on their face though.

Pie face

January 23 is National Pie Day. People cook up and gobble down pies of every kind. There are pie-eating and pie-throwing competitions where folks can scoff a pie, plant their face in a pie, or hurl a pie. Let's hope no one up-chucks a pie, or it'll be a real mess fest!

Big boy

When Bob Wian made the first double-decker burger in 1936, customers couldn't get enough of it. One fan was a chubby six-year-old who helped sweep up at the shop for a free burger. Bob named his new burger after his young pal and the famous BigBoy was born.

September 12 is National Chocolate Milkshake Day.

Drive-ins and drive-throughs

We think it's normal to bark orders from a car window to a box and have it talk back to us! The first drive-through was built in California in 1948. Today, you can even drive through doughnut holes to order food!

WANT MORE?

Check out the champs at Major League Eating ★ **www.ifoce.com/records.php**

GAME'S ON

Eyes are focused. Hearts are racing. More than 111 million sports fans are on the edge of their seats. It's Super Bowl Sunday! The game is on, and so is almost every TV in the country. Football fans flock to watch their heroes play ball. But the biggest players may be the commercials. A 30-second spot of airtime can cost a cool $3.5 million!

Hair-raising tactics
Troy Polamalu of the Pittsburgh Steelers is an outstanding player with outstanding hair. In 2010 his locks were insured for $1 million. Let's hope they're not hair today, gone tomorrow!

PERHAPS I CAN SNAG THE BALL WITH MY LEGENDARY LOCKS!

700,000 footballs are made each year for the NFL.

The gear
Helmets, face masks, and pads provide protection for players. Linemen are padded to the max because they do the most blocking and tackling.

Around 11 million lb (5 million kg) of potato chips are eaten by fans during the game.

ON THE WILD SIDE

Sports can bring out the animal in everyone, but many American football teams are fierce and feral. Check out these wild team names, and those of their mascots:

- ★ Atlanta Falcons—Freddie
- ★ Buffalo Bills—Billy Buffalo
- ★ Carolina Panthers—Sir Purr
- ★ Chicago Bears—Staley da Bear
- ★ Denver Broncos—Miles
- ★ Detroit Lions—Roary
- ★ Philadelphia Eagles—Swoop
- ★ St. Louis Rams—Rampage!

HAIR? I'M MORE WORRIED ABOUT MY TEETH!

The Yell Squad

No big game is complete without chants and pom-poms. The first cheerleading team was started in 1903 by a bunch of men (yes, men!) who called themselves "The Yell Squad."

HOPE WE GET WINTER UNIFORMS NEXT YEAR.

WANT MORE?

National Football League ★ www.nfl.com/superbowl

EXPLORING'S NOT FOR WIMPS

Meriwether Lewis was an intrepid explorer, a nature nut, and more often than not, a magnet for misadventure! In 1804, with fellow explorer William Clark, he led the famous Lewis and Clark expedition into the unmapped wilds west of the Mississippi. A new era of exploration had begun in 1803, thanks to what may be the best real estate deal in history—the Louisiana Purchase. It doubled the area of the United States for less than three cents an acre!

Just bluffing?

Lewis mapped many new places, treading where few would dare to go. If he'd had a bungee cord, his habit of falling off cliffs may not have been so heart-stopping! Instead of bouncing back, Lewis escaped death more than once by thrusting his dagger into a cliff and hauling himself to safety.

BULLSEYE!

When exploring wild woods wearing buckskins, it's best not to be accompanied by a near-sighted hunting partner. Lewis was shot in the buttocks by one-eyed expedition member Pierre Cruzatte, who mistook his captain for an elk. That was the boss' derrière, Pierre!

William Clark

Meriwether Lew

HE DOES LOOK A BIT LIKE AN ELK IN THAT COAT.

OH, DEER!

Sacagawea was the only woman who traveled with the explorers.

FORT CLATSOP

Cascade Range

Rocky

Lewis's Route

Great

FORT MANDAN

Clark's Route

GREAT FALLS

POMPY'S TOWER

Mountains

Plains

START

ST. LOUIS

KEY

— Outward journey
May 1804–November 1805

Λ Return journey
March–September 1806

■ The Louisiana Purchase
April 30, 1803

I CAN'T BEAR TO BE BREAKFAST FOR A BEAR!

A bear behind

The explorers kept journals. They encountered and documented many animals they had never seen before. Of these, grizzly bears were by far the most frightening. Lewis almost met a grizzly end himself when one decided to chase him.

WANT MORE?

Relive the journey through the journals ☆ lewis-clark.org

SIZE IT UP

There's no getting around it. Americans think BIG—especially about monuments and memorials. Look at the line up of legendary leaders with their stony stares carved multiple stories high into the granite cliffs of South Dakota, for example.

TAKE THAT, MOUNT RUSHMORE!

Another giant face emerges from the stone in South Dakota. It's a memorial to Crazy Horse, who was a famous Native American leader. The job commenced in 1948 and is still going on. This will be the world's largest sculpture when it's finished. Crazy!

Crazy Horse's stone head will be 90ft (27m) high!

George Washington

I'M STARTING TO CRACK UNDER THE STRAIN!

Thomas Jefferson

Theodore Roosevelt

Big boys
Presidents often seem larger than life, especially the fantastic four at Mount Rushmore. George Washington's head is as high as a five-story building!

LETTING OFF STEAM

Where could you blow your stack, burst your boiler, and scrape your bottom all at once? Aboard a steamboat on the Mississippi River during the 1800s, of course! People call this rolling river with its magnificent mile-wide tide the "Big Muddy." Barges and tugs ferry freight along the great inland waterway today, but steamboats and showboats once smoked and whistled their way along, and sometimes under!

Waterskiing was invented on the Mississippi River in 1922.

The Delta Queen

A sinking feeling

In 1925, when the steamer *ME Norman* sank, an African-American river worker named Tom Lee Park made a splash when he rescued 32 panicked people from drowning. A memorial was erected to honor his brave act. River rescue was a case of not diving in in the deep end for Tom, though—he couldn't swim!

That's the spirit

Stories of spooky sightings surround the *Delta Queen*. Her owner, the legendary Ma Greene, didn't approve of alcohol being sold on her boat, so when a saloon opened onboard after her death in 1949, Ma's ghost began dishing out trouble with the drinks!

esky pirates

oats can hit a snag along
ne Mississippi, but nature is not
lways to blame. Samuel Mason led
gang of river pirates. He would
ffer to guide boats through
roublesome waters, then run them
ground near his gang of raiders.

ARR, LET ME TAKE YER TO A NICE RESTING PLACE!

IT'S NOTHING TO GET ALL STEAMED UP ABOUT!

FAST-FLOW FACTS

★ The name Mississippi comes from the Ojibwe Indians who called the river "Mee-zee-see-bee," or Father of the Waters.

★ The river starts as a trickle from Lake Itasca in Minnesota and flows 2,340mi (3,766km) to the Gulf of Mexico.

★ A raindrop falling at Lake Itasca would arrive at the Gulf of Mexico in about 90 days.

★ Huge earthquakes in Missouri in December 1811 to February 1812 caused the Mississippi River to flow backward!

ANYONE WANT TO PLAY EYE-SPY?

Alligator eyeballs

Alligators laze about in the muddy river waters. The best way to keep an eye on alligator populations is by boat at night. Officials count the alligator eyeballs, which shine bright red in the darkness.

WANT MORE?

Enjoy a song and a whistle with showboats and calliopes ★ www.steamboats.org

SHOW ME THE MONEY

This stuff has been called "dough," "beans," "bucks," "smackers," "greenbacks," and "cha-chingers." It's money. Hard to earn, easy to spend. Sometimes won, sometimes lost. In the United States today, the highest value note you could have in your wallet is $100, but long ago you could have had a whopping $100,000 bill stashed away—you wouldn't want to see that piece of paper go down the drain, would you?

THE REAL DEAL

In the United States about one in every 12,500 dollars is counterfeit. Some features have been added to the notes to make them more difficult to forge:

* A security thread running from top to bottom
* A watermark of the same person as the note's portrait
* Color-shifting ink which appears to change color when the note is tilted
* Micro-printing

The average dollar bill has a lifespan of about 18-22 months.

Faking it
Crooks were once sentenced to death for making bogus bill or counterfeiting. There are an estimated 70 million counterfe dollars doing the rounds today Take note of your notes.

QUITE FRANKLY, THERE ARE NO GAINS WITHOUT PAINS.

NONE OF THAT FAKE STUFF FOR ME, THANKS.

HMM, WHEN WILL THEY PUT MY FACE ON A NOTE?

I CAN'T MAKE HEAD NOR TAIL OF THESE COINS!

Penny, nickel, dime, quarter
A penny is worth one cent. The first penny was designed in 1787 by Benjamin Franklin. A nickel is five cents, a dime is ten cents, and a quarter is 25 cents—make sense?

buried treasure
old bars are a form of money called bullion. The ation's greatest stockpile f bullion lies in a vault nder Manhattan. It's a ase of bars behind bars!

MONEY MATTERS

NYSE—New York Stock Exchange, where deals are wheeled, shares are bought and sold, and fortunes rise or fall.

Wall Street—a narrow street in New York City and the heart of banking and business.

Wall Street bull—a 3.5 ton (3,200kg) bronze sculpture of a charging bull symbolizing financial strength and power.

Bull and bear markets—when share prices are rising, it is called a "bull market," for a bull strikes upward with its horns. When they are falling, it is called a "bear market," for a bear slashes downward with its paws.

The Great Depression—a time in the 1930s when the US economy was paralyzed, stock markets crashed, banks failed, businesses went bankrupt, and many people lost their jobs.

WANT MORE?

Who was the first president on a coin? ☆ www.usmint.gov

KEEPING THE FAITH

Can you imagine living without computers, cell phones, and a car? For the Amish, their faith calls for a simple way of life that sets them apart from the hustle and bustle of the outside world. Horse-drawn carriages are the main means of transportation in Amish communities, where it is forbidden to own a car.

Hairy matters

Amish men do not shave their beards once they are married, but mustaches are a definite no-no. Women never cut their hair. They part it down the middle and wear it in a bun beneath their prayer caps.

Stolen quilts

Many Amish women sew beautiful handcrafted quilts. The Amish began selling their popular quilts to the public when they noticed they were being stolen from clotheslines!

RUMSPRINGA WILL CERTAINLY PUT A SPRING IN MY STEP!

Rumspringa

Most Amish children are schooled until eighth grade. At about sixteen years of age, Amish youths are released from the rules of the church and community to experience life among the non-Amish. This time of decision-making and dating is called "rumspringa."

HOPE I DON'T RUN OUT OF GAS BEFORE I FINISH THIS.

NO POCKETS? WHERE WILL I PUT MY IPHONE?

Off the grid

The Amish choose not to be connected to the electrical power grid. They use gas, batteries, generators, or oil to power machines, tools, and home appliances.

No little secrets

There are no pockets in Amish clothing. This is to avoid the temptation of having secret treasures tucked away that could make one person feel special.

THE PLAIN PEOPLE

The Amish, Mennonite, and Brethren communities in the United States are known as the "Plain People." Not because they live on the prairies, but because they wear simple clothes and live and worship in plain buildings. The largest Amish communities are in Holmes County, Ohio and Lancaster County, Pennsylvania.

WANT MORE?

Questions and answers about Amish life ✭ www.amish.net/faq.asp

ROPES, REINS, AND RODEOS

Imagine strutting about in baggy britches and checking your makeup before facing a furious freight train of a bull! That's all in a day's work for bullfighters known as rodeo clowns. When the chute opens, the raging bull bucks, and the rider bites the dust. A rodeo clown swings into action with outrageous antics to distract the bull so the sore-bottomed cowboy can scramble to safety!

IT'S NOT ALWAYS A BARREL OF LAUGHS!

Clown lounge
Rodeo clowns do dangerous work. The barrel in the center of a rodeo arena is a safe refuge—called a "clown lounge." A clown can sit tight in the barrel then pop up to distract the bull.

COME HERE, STEER. DON'T BE A BIG BULLY!

ANOTHER ONE BITES THE DUST! BYE-BYE COWBOY.

Gory glory
Rodeo bulls leave the arena unharmed, but that is not always the case for cowboys and clowns. Broken bones and backside bruises come with the thrills and spills.

ROUND-UP ON THE RANCH

Rodeo developed during the 1800s when cowboys would show off their skills in bronco riding and steer roping at the ranch after a cattle drive or round-up. Today, huge crowds gather to watch cowboys and cowgirls compete.

THIS IS NO TIME FOR HORSING AROUND!

LEARN THE LINGO

buckaroo

lasso

bronco

stampede

rodeo

Many cowboys came from Mexico, so many Wild West words come from Spanish. Match each word to its meaning:

A: a sudden rush of horses or cattle

D: a wild, untamed horse

C: a rope with a noose at one end

B: a cow handler

E: a contest to show cowboy skills

Answers: buckaroo=B; lasso=C; bronco=D; stampede=A; rodeo=E

I WANT MY MAA-MA!

Mutton bustin'
Some rodeo stars are born to ride. Three-year-olds have a wild and woolly start on sheep. They can try riding steers by the age of six. Let's hope they don't get too big for their britches!

WANT MORE?

Find out about the rodeos, the wranglers, and the big prizes ☆ www.prorodeo.com

TALES FROM THE RAILS

Trains have huffed, puffed, belched, and tooted their way across the country. When the lure of land pulled people west, railroad companies raced to lay down tracks from coast to coast. America's first transcontinental railroad slashed travel time from a snail-paced six months to a triumphant ten days, although fires, derailments, and breakdowns were hair-raising hazards along the way!

Thanks mainly to rail timetables, there are four time zones across the continental USA (Pacific, Mountain, Central, Eastern)

> IT'S A PARTY. C'MON, DO THE LOCOMOTION WITH ME!

THE GOLDEN SPIKE

It was love at first sight when the rail line from the east met the rail line from the west! The world's first transcontinental railroad was done and dusted when the last and "golden" spike was driven in at Promontory, Utah, on May 10, 1869.

I'VE GOT THE WRONG END OF THE STICK. WAIT, IS THIS DYNAMITE?

I'M ALL PUFFED OUT FROM WATCHING THEM WORK SO HARD!

Working on the railroad

More than 12,000 Chinese immigrants helped build America's first transcontinental railroad. They were poorly paid and often railroaded into handling the most dangerous tasks, such as blasting tunnels.

Iron horses and buffalo bullies

The pointed wedge at the front of an early train is a "cow catcher." It pushed animals away so the train could stay on the tracks. It was fatal for the buffalo, who stood even less of a chance when passengers took potshots at them from the windows. Were these the first "bullet" trains?

The ten-mile day

Crews from the Central Pacific and the Union Pacific Railroad Companies worked at full steam to lay the last miles of track. Charles Crocker of the Central Railroad bet $10,000 that his men could lay an unheard of 10mi (16km) of track in a single day! They did AND set a world record that remains unbroken to this day.

10 MILES OF TRACK, LAID IN ONE DAY. APRIL 28TH 1869

WANT MORE?

STARS AND STRIPES

In the early years, people almost couldn't see the stars for the stripes on the US flag! A star and a stripe were added each time a state joined the Union. By 1818 Congress got in a bit of a flap and decided that the flag should have only 13 stripes—one for each of the original colonies. Each of the 50 states is represented by a star, making the flag truly "star-spangled."

"The Star-Spangled Banner" is one name for the US flag. It's also called "Stars and Stripes" and "Old Glory."

Battles and bombs

The flag had fighting spirit from the start. It was made to fly over Fort McHenry, the site of a beastly battle against the British. It was to be big enough so that the British would have no trouble seeing it over the bombs!

O SAY, CAN YOU SEE ... WHAT I SEE?

Battle at Fort McHenry

I'M FEELING VERY STARRY-EYED OVER ALL THIS!

FOLDING THE FLAG

There's a traditional way to fold the flag that produces a triangle showing only the stars and the blue field, or union, behind them:

1. Open the flag to full length. Fold the flag lengthwise.

2. Fold lengthwise again until only half the blue field and about three stripes show.

3. Fold one stripe-end corner to the edge, creating a triangle fold.

4. Fold the new pointed end over the flag again.

5. Continue the triangle folds for the length of the flag.

6. Fold the blue field over itself and tuck the end of the flag into the last fold.

Super-sized flag

Thomas "Ski" Demski must have really been seeing stars when he had a record-shattering Star-Spangled Banner sewn for Flag Day on June 14 in 1992. It took 500 people to unfurl the flag, which measured a whopping 505ft by 225ft (154m x 68.5m)!

I WAS THINKING OF FOLDING IT UP, BUT NOW I'M FLAGGING.

WANT MORE?

Investigate the flag and the song ☆ americanhistory.si.edu/starspangledbanner

STREET BEAT

Today, rappers battle with lightning-fast lyrics, and hip-hop dancers pop, lock, strobe, and krump to the beat. Hip-hop grew up in the Bronx during the 1970s, where pioneers like DJ Kool Herc would tap into power lines to connect speakers and turntables and perform for free at street parties. The bling came later!

Rapping is known as MCing, from the initials for Master of Ceremonies.

Snoop Doggy Dogg
Calvin Cordozar Broadus, Jr. got his nickname from his mother because his eyes reminded her of Snoopy, the cartoon dog from Charlie Brown. Rumor has it that Snoop D-O-Double-G loves cats. Isn't dat a swizzle!

OOPS! I THINK I JUST HEARD MY PANTS RIP.

Speedy syllables

Speed rapper Busta Rhymes made it into the Guinness Book of World Records in 2000 for having said the most syllables in one second!

PSST, DON'T TELL ANYONE, BUT MY REAL NAME'S TREVOR SMITH!

Hip means "in the know." Hop is a dance move. Put them together and you have hip-hop.

KERCHING, BLING

Hip hop stars are often draped, or "iced out," in flashy bling, such as chunky gold chains, jewelled dogtags, doorknocker earrings, and even silver or gold tooth caps, called "grillz."

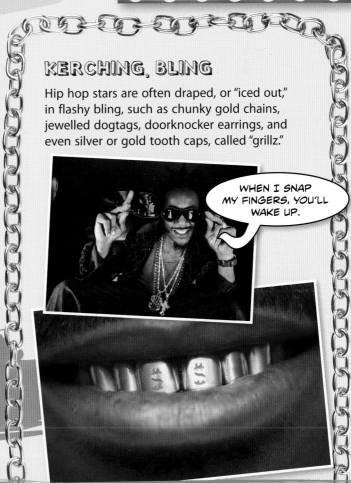

WHEN I SNAP MY FINGERS, YOU'LL WAKE UP.

uperstar singer

issy "Misdemeanor" Elliott ways wanted to be a superstar nger. As a four-year-old, she ould sing to her doll babies d make them clap for her! issy is one of hip-hop's top male artists—those baby lls knew their stuff.

WANT MORE?

DUST BOWL TO FRUIT BOWL

America's worst dust storm grew out of the blue on April 14, 1935—a day people call Black Sunday. It sent 5 million acres (2 million hectares) of dirt spinning across the land, turning the sky into inky blackness. During a decade known as the "dirty thirties," much of the Great Plains was devastated by a series of deadly dust storms. The area was called the Dust Bowl, and families fled west to California to find a better life.

WE'RE LAYING AROUND TILL THE DUST SETTLES!

In a flap
The day can turn as black as night during a dust storm. Chickens got mixed up and went to roost during the day.

Dust bunnies
A plague of ravenous rabbits wreaked havoc on the ruined farms. People were forced to shoot and eat them. With no greens in sight, pickled tumbleweed was one of the only available side dishes.

UH-OH, I'M IN A BIT OF A PICKLE!

I'LL JUST POP IN AND BUY A FACE MASK...

Nasty nibblers
Tarantulas, centipedes, grasshoppers, and crickets swarmed over the dust-caked land. They gobbled up almost everything—even the wooden handles of shovels and other tools!

ROUTE 66

Dust Bowl refugees were known as "Okies," even though not all of them came from Oklahoma. Route 66 took them to greener pastures—and hopefully to a better future—in California.

Areas affected by dust storms

California

Route 66

Heart of the Dust Bowl

Different states had different coloured dust:
Kansas dust--black,
Oklahoma dust--red,
Texas dust--yellow.

Getaway car
People packed themselves and their possessions into their jalopies—that's an old, beat-up car—and headed west.

SIMON SAYS... HANDS ON HEADS!

HANG ON TO YOUR HAT!

Stories from the Dust Bowl:

⭐ LeRoy Hankel watched the wind from a dust storm blow a truck 30ft (10m) down the street.

⭐ Ellroy Hoffman had planted alfalfa seeds. When a dust storm came up, it blew the seeds right out of the ground!

⭐ Harvey Pickrel bought a tractor for next to nothing. But it was nearly totally buried in dust and he had to dig it out first.

WANT MORE?

Kids wore dust masks to school! ⭐ www.english.illinois.edu/maps/depression/dustbowl.htm

THE BRIDGE THAT COULDN'T BE BUILT?

It was a long shot. The bridge would span a stormy strait. It would be hit by strong ocean currents, shrouded in fog, and whipped by fierce winds. After the perilous project got the green light in 1924, construction was delayed so often many called it "the bridge that couldn't be built." Wrong! Despite the suspense, San Francisco's world-famous Golden Gate Bridge opened in 1937.

I'M SO HUNGRY I COULD EAT MY HARD-BOILED HAT!

Safety ahead
A hard-boiled hat was the first kind of protective headgear for bridge workers. Early hard hats were made out of steamed canvas, glue, and black paint!

Commemorative plaque marks the 25th anniversary

Panicky pigeons
In 1933, 250 carrier pigeons were released to carry the news that construction had started. But the pigeons were so frightened by the crowds that they hid in the exhibition model of the bridge and had to be shooed out by boys with sticks!

Saved by the net

Nineteen men could have plummeted to their death during construction, but they were saved by a revolutionary safety net suspended beneath the deck from end to end. The lucky lads became known as the "Half-Way-to-Hell Club!"

IN SUSPENSE

The Golden Gate Bridge spans 8,981ft (2,737m) and is held up by cables slung from two tall towers. Enough steel wire was used in the cables to circle the planet three times.

High-viz

Golden Gate Bridge is painted in an outstanding color. The high-visibility "International Orange" makes it easier for passing ships to see it in dense fog.

WANT MORE?

FREEDOM HIGHWAY

There's nothing like the roar of a ready engine, a full tank of gas, and an open stretch of road ahead. Rambling byways and high-speed highways slice through deserts and prairies, skirt canyons, climb rocky mountain passes, streak across state borders, and criss-cross great cities. There are often new sights to see around each bend and the promise of adventure on the horizon. Of course, your GPS may go haywire, the highway patrol may be lurking, and if you're road-tripping with the top down, try not to smile or you'll get bugs in your teeth!

Most car horns have perfect pitch! They play the note "F."

Speed demons
In 1898 the NYPD used bicycles to chase down speeding motorists! Today, some 34 million speeding tickets are issued each year.

What a stretch

There are super-stretch Hummer limos, custom motorbike limos, and speedy racing limos, but the longest limo of all has 26 tires and measures more than 98ft (30m) from hood to trunk. What a road hog!

Model A, B, C, or T?

Thanks to Henry Ford, his automobile assembly line, and the affordable Model T, many Americans could buy their own wheels. Ford produced models A, B, C, F, K, N, R, and S before the Model T hit the road in 1908.

WE MAKE A MODEL COUPLE IN OUR MODEL T!

ROAD CODE

With the age of the automobile, many new words and phrases were invented. Some have traveled through time. Others have fallen by the roadside. Match each word to its meaning:

1 AUTOBUBBLING
2 GAS GUZZLER
3 RATTLETRAP
4 ROAD HOG
5 ROAD RAGE
6 STEP ON THE GAS

Meanings:

A a driver who blocks the road

B to go on a drive just for fun

C a car that uses a lot of fuel

D to accelerate

E anger caused by other motorists

F a rickety old car

Answers: 1=B; 2=C; 3=F; 4=A; 5=E; 6=D

THIS WAS SUPPOSED TO BE A FINE DAY FOR A DRIVE, NOT A FINE. IT'S HIGHWAY ROBBERY!

WANT MORE?

Go along for the ride on America's first road trip ☆ **www.pbs.org/horatio/about**

BEAUTY QUEENS

What in the world is a "wiglet?" Are fake-teeth "flippers" applied before or after the perfect spray tan? And just how many sparkling, semi-precious stones can one to-die-for dress handle? Knowing the answers to these questions may nudge the contestants who enter the arena of glitz pageants a little closer to the limelight, but it is often stage presence, personality, and poise that bag the biggest prizes in the world of beauty queens.

Grinning and winning
Even teeth can gleam and glow when beauty pageant contestants wear a set of detachable dental veneers known as a "flipper" for a totally winning smile.

IF I DON'T WIN, I'LL SCREAM!

Parades and pageants
The first Miss America Beauty Pageant was held in Atlantic City in 1921. Today, beauty pageants and parades are held across the country. Some young contestants are barely as tall as the terrific trophies they win!

Key to the crown
Some contestants have a coach to teach them how to pose, what to wear, how to do their hair and makeup, and what to say in the interview. What do you say about that?

I FORGOT THE QUESTION!

Showman PT Barnum staged the first beauty contest in 1855. He also organized shows for bullfrogs, poultry, and cats!

WHAT'S IN A PAGEANT KIT?

Jewelry, false eyelashes, fake nails, nail glue, flipper, glue gun, hair straightener, curling iron, hairspray, hair extensions, wiglet (that's a small wig, not a wig for a piglet!), makeup, body glitter… and more!

First and shortest
Margaret Gorman became the first Miss America in 1921. At 5ft 1in (155cm) she was also the shortest. During the competition, some of her rivals daringly wore bare-legged bathing suits.

WANT MORE?

Get the shows and the charities ☆ www.missuniverse.com/missusa

WELCOME TO *Fabulous* **LAS VEGAS** NEVADA

SAYING "I DO" IN VEGAS

If you dream of a white wedding that is also weird, wild, wacky, or tacky, Las Vegas is the place to say "I Do" any way you want to. This neon-flashing mega-playground is often called the "Wedding Capital of the World." Some crazy couples don't even get out of their car! One chapel has a drive-through window. Others offer themed weddings— hey, is Elvis about to run away with the bride?

Dream themes
Vegas is honeymoon heaven. Why go to Paris, Venice, or New York City, when you can find the Eiffel Tower, gondolas, and the Statue of Liberty right here?

In Vegas, some 315 love-struck couples say "I Do" every single day.

Just Married

Chapels of love
There are wedding chapels along the Las Vegas Strip and in many hotels. The real Elvis was married in Vegas in 1967. Cupid's Wedding Chapel now has two Elvises for couples to choose from!

Cupid's WEDDING CHAPEL

LOVE

8

OUR ELVIS IS PRETTIER THAN YOUR ELVIS!

I HOPE YOU RECOGNIZE EACH OTHER, 'COS I CAN'T SEE A THING!

HITTING THE JACKPOT

Kerching! Vegas weddings are not always cheap. But if you won the highest slot machine jackpot ever hit, you'd have almost $40 million! That'd pay for a honeymoon, too.

Whacky weddings
In Vegas, couples can be married by Darth Vader, Merlin the Magician, or Elvis! They can get hitched underwater, aboard a pirate ship, or in midair doing a bungee jump.

WANT MORE?

It lies in the desert, but the name Las Vegas means "The Meadows" in Spanish.

What does a furry little rodent and a hill called Gobbler's Knob have to do with the weather? A big deal, according to followers of a famous groundhog named Punxsutawney Phil. Each February 2 for more than 100 years, fat Phil has been pulled out of his heated burrow beneath a fake tree stump onto center stage to make his powerful prediction. If the sun is out and Phil spots his shadow, he'll turn tail and dive into his burrow. To the top-hat-clad officials and Phil's fans on Groundhog Day, that means six more weeks of winter!

They say, "If the sun shines on Groundhog Day, half the fuel and half the hay."

IS THAT A LOAD OF HOGWASH?

PHIL'S FEARLESS FORECAST

OH PHIL, WHAT BIG TEETH YOU HAVE... DON'T YOU DARE BITE ME!

I'M A GRUMPYHOG. I'M SUPPOSED TO BE HIBERNATIN'!

Woodchuck whittling and more
As many as 30,000 fans flock to Punxsutawney in Pennsylvania for Groundhog Day celebrations. There are sleigh rides, ice-carving competitions, and even a chance to do some woodchuck whittling!

People call me the Weather Prophet Extraordinaire!

YOU LOOK MIGHTY FINE FOR AN OLD HOG, PHIL.

THANK YOU, PHYLLIS, BUT I'M FEELING A BIT UNDER THE WEATHER.

die but goodie

nxsutawney's resident
dent, Phil, is long-lived for
marmot. Many say this is
anks to his fabulous furry
ife, Phyllis, and sips of secret
roundhog Punch!

Mad hatters

The chaps in top hats who lead the
Punxsutawney Phil ceremony are known
as the "Inner Circle." They take care of Phil
all year. Phil tells them his prediction in a
special language called "groundhogese."

FESTIVALS AND FUN

The promise of spring is one reason to
celebrate, but there is a feast of festivals
and traditions all year long. Read the clues
to figure out the fun:

☆ This special day for sweethearts features
   love hearts, love letters, and candy galore.
☆ People parade in masks and costumes
   for this crazy carnival in New Orleans.
☆ There are stars, stripes, food, and
   fireworks all around for this big holiday.
☆ On this night of fright, tricksters roam
   the streets for treats.

* Valentine's Day (February 14)
* Mardi Gras (around Easter)
* Independence Day (July 4)
* Halloween (October 31)

WANT MORE?

Find out about Phil's perfect predictions ☆ www.stormfax.com/ghogday.htm

UNDERCOVER SOLDIERS

They traded their hoop skirts and killer corsets for ill-fitting uniforms. They stained their faces, perhaps attached a false mustache, and gave their long hair the chop. But these gals could shoot a gun as accurately as the best of the lads. Hundreds of brave women disguised themselves as men so they could join the fighting forces in the American Civil War.

> I'M JUST CHECKING HOW STRONG YOUR TEETH ARE.

A WINNING SMILE

Doctors examined recruits, but luckily for women warriors, not too closely. Soldiers had to use their teeth to rip open gun cartridges, so candidates could enter the ranks simply by having a good set of chompers. Smile!

Man, it's Melverina!

In addition to handling a rifle like a pro, Melverina Elverina Peppercorn was a woman who could spit tobacco 10ft (3m) high! Perhaps this helped her slip into the Confederate Army disguised as a man so she could fight alongside her twin brother, Lexy.

> I SPY WITH MY LITTLE EYE...

Sarah Edmonds was a spy and nurse in the Union Army. She used many disguises, male and female!

Beardless boys

Sneaky women soldiers didn't have to pretend to shave because boys often fought, too. Soldiers had to be 18. But some younger boys wrote "18" on a piece of paper and put it in their shoe so they could truthfully say they were "over 18!"

Don't mess with this wife

One gutsy gal named Malinda Blalock joined the fighting forces with her husband, only she signed up as his brother, Sam. Officials soon learned Sam was a super cook, so "he" was assigned as the unit's Mess Wife—how true!

THE CIVIL WAR

The Civil War began on April 12, 1861. The conflict was over slavery.

★ Many in the South believed America's 4 million slaves were necessary for business.

★ Many in the North believed that it was wrong and cruel to keep people as slaves.

★ General Ulysses S. Grant led the northern Union forces; General Robert E. Lee led the southern Confederate Army.

★ The Civil War ended in 1865 and slavery was outlawed.

Grant (left) and Lee work out terms for the surrender of Lee's army.

HOW DO YOU SPELL "SURRENDER?"

WANT MORE?

About 620,000 soldiers died in the Civil War ★ www.nps.gov/civilwar

SURFER SUPREME

Try saying "Duke Paoa Kahinu Mokoe Hulikohola Kahanamoku" without coming up for air! Luckily, most people call him "Duke." His friends say he had fins for feet. And his hands were so big that when he scooped up water and threw it, it was like being drenched by the bucketload! Duke was born in Hawaii in 1890. Known as the "father of modern surfing," he rode his big wooden board on Hawaii's waves and carved out a sport that swept the world off its feet.

Un-useful fact: Duke was named aft[er] his father, who w[as] named after the Du[ke] of Edinburgh!

Worldwide ride

Duke introduced surfing to the world. He didn't have a board with him when he toured Australia in 1915, so he made one out of sugar pine. His demo was so dynamic, even the sharks were left gasping! Today, statues in Oahu and Sydney honor the great Duke.

Sink or swim

When Duke was a little boy, his father and uncle took him out to sea in an outrigger canoe and threw him into the surf! It was sink or swim, in the true Hawaiian way. Naturally, young Duke rose to the occasion.

SURFER SPEAK

If you want to be a ripper (that's a really hot surfer),
you could add to the act by learning the lingo!
Match each word to its meaning:

shark biscuit

shredding

grom

barrel

nose

A: a boogie boarder

B: the pointy part of a surfboard

C: a hollow wave

D: a young surfer

E: surfing really well on a wave

Answers: shark biscuit=A; shredding=E; grom=D; barrel=C; nose=B

HELP! I SHOULD HAVE TAKEN UP MARBLES!

Monster waves
Hawaii has some of the most famous surf beaches in the world. Giant waves, nicknamed "bluebirds," sweep into the shores. Expert surfers are towed out on jet skis to brave the breakers.

WANT MORE?

Duke's remarkable life ☆ www.dukeswaikiki.com/duke

SLED DOG DELIVERY

Imagine needing life-saving medicine—and fast! Trouble is, you're in the tiny, snowbound town of Nome in an isolated part of Alaska, it's blizzard season, and the only possible delivery service is by dog sled. Enter Balto. In 1925 this smart, big-hearted Siberian husky led a team of sled dogs on the final leg of a 1,000mi (1,609km) mission to deliver medicine that would save the children of Nome. Doggie Doc's here—WOOF!

Balto the sled dog with musher Gunnar Kassen

A do-or-die dilemma
Diphtheria can be deadly. Pack ice stopped ships getting through. Blizzards stopped planes. A train carried the medicine part way. Then it all went to the dogs!

WE'RE ALL BARKING MAD, BUT WE DID IT!

The life-saving medicine arrives in Nome after seven days.

Mush, mush
Passing medicine from one relay team to another was like playing "hot potato." More than 20 sled drivers, called mushers (not mashers), and their teams took part in the doggy-express to Nome.

Blinding blizzards
Alaska's not the place for a tropical vacation! Almost a third of it lies north of the Arctic Circle. Winter temps rarely rise above −40°F (−40°C) and howling winds can knock over dogs and sleds.

LIFE OR DEATH RACE

The legend of Balto lives on. Every year since 1973, the Iditarod Trail Sled Dog Race has run from Anchorage to Nome to honor the relay of 1925 and Alaska's dog sled teams. By the end of the 9- to 15-day race, contestants must feel like death warmed up!

> WE'RE PRETTY CHILLED AT THE MOMENT.

> In mid-winter parts of Alaska receive only about four to five hours of daylight.

> I WISH I WAS A DOG WITH A BONE!

Bronze statue of Balto in NYC's Central Park

Last leg
Racing in white-out conditions, Balto led the way home to Nome. The dogs were on their last legs when they arrived. Balto was a hero. Hope he got a doggie bag!

WANT MORE?

ISLANDS OF HOPE

Many Americans are descended from immigrants who arrived with the hope of building a bright future. Men, women, and children trickled in during the 1600s but by the mid-1800s, families were flooding in. To control the flow, a tiny island in New York Harbor was chosen as an immigration station. But who would pass the excruciating examinations at Ellis Island?

In the early 1900s, a children's playground was created on the roof of the main building at Ellis Island.

> HELLO AND GOODBYE.

FIT ENOUGH TO STAY?

☆ Not if you coughed, sneezed, wheezed, or limped.

☆ Not if you failed the test of the "button-hook men" who checked for eye disease by flipping eyelids inside out with a hairpin or a button-hook. OUCH!

☆ If you seemed sick, you were marked with blue chalk and sent home or hospitalized.

Key to chalk marks:

B = back
E = eyes
SC = scalp
C = conjunctivitis
FT = feet
N = neck
H = heart
F = face

I WONDER IF THIS PHOTOGRAPHER IS MARRIED.

ANGEL ISLAND

Ellis Island, on the east coast of the United States, opened as an immigration station in 1892 and processed mainly European migrants. Angel Island, off San Francisco, opened in 1910 and was known as the "Ellis Island of the West." Of the migrants processed there, 97% were from China.

Love Boat
In 1907 the SS *Baltic* sailed into New York with 1,000 single women on board, each looking for a husband. It's rumored that some got married in the Great Hall, before even leaving Ellis Island. Now that's keen!

Immigration peaked in 1907
1,285,349
and plunged in 1933 (the Depression)
23,068

IT'S DARK AND LONELY IN HERE NOW.

Family connections
Around half the people in the United States today can trace their roots to a family member who came through Ellis Island. This could explain why 3 million people each year now visit the Immigration Museum there.

...st man out
...nnie Moore, a 14-year-old ...om Ireland, was the first ...migrant processed at Ellis ...and. In 1954 Norwegian ...aman Arne Peterssen was ...e last. Hope he didn't forget ...turn out the lights!

DO YOU THINK I LOOK LIKE HER?

WANT MORE?

Search for famous arrivals at Ellis Island ✭ **www.ellisisland.org**

CANDY BAR KING

People say money melts away, but what if you were paid in chocolate? The Aztec Indians were first to twig onto the treasures of the cacao tree. They bashed the beans to make a chocolate beverage fit for kings. Centuries later, a sweetie named Milton Hershey cracked the recipe to give Americans a chocolate bar so cheap they could afford the treat even if they barely had a bean!

> I'M SWEET ON THE OUTSIDE, BUT INSIDE I'M A BIT NUTS!

> THIS IS SUCH A SWEET BUSINESS.

A nutter for peanut butter

People thought that coating bite-size morsels of peanut butter in chocolate was an out-of-this-world idea—even E.T. the alien thought Reese's Pieces were worth phoning home about!

KISS AND TELL

Milton Hershey built a town around his chocolate factory in Pennsylvania. In Hershey, the streets have names like Chocolate Avenue, and the lampost lights are shaped like kisses, but it all started with cacao beans in the jungle.

> LOOK OUT, THAT'S NOT A CHOCOLATE PIE, IT'S A COW PIE!

hocolate drops
hocolate tastes heavenly,
ut can it fall from the sky?
es! In 1948, in the aftermath
f World War II, a US Air Force
lot nicknamed "The Chocolate
ier" parachuted chocolate bars
om his C-54 plane to children
war-torn Berlin.

WE'RE FEELING
A BIT SHATTERED
BY NOW.

I'M HAVING
A MELTDOWN!

BUT SOON
WE'LL BE
TOTALLY WRAPPED!

WANT
MORE?

It's chocolate time! ✭ www.mce.k12tn.net/chocolate/history/name.htm

TORTURE YOUR TASTE BUDS

Some foods are simply too hot to handle. Try a red-hot chili pepper, for example. One bite can cause pain and suffering. The mouth is on fire, the eyes water, and the best remedy, they say, is to eat more. No way, José! Other traditional American foods just tickle your taste buds instead of fry them.

The almighty peanut
The average American kid will eat 1,500 peanut butter and jelly sandwiches by the time they graduate from high school. Americans are nutters for peanut butter. Each year, they eat enough of it to cover the floor of the Grand Canyon!

THAT SOUNDS NUTS!

A-MAIZE-ing
Native Americans have been popping corn for thousands of years and they didn't even have movies back then! Some thought that spirits lived inside the kernels. These got angrier as their homes were heated, and finally burst out in a cranky puff of steam.

THIS IS A SUREFIRE WAY TO ZAP MY APPETITE!

READY, AIM, FIRE!

There are more than 100 varieties of chili peppers. Some taste sweet, some are mild, but some will send you through the roof. And it's usually the littlest ones you have to look out for! Most of the heat of a chili is in the seeds and the veins. So handle with care and follow these hot tips:

⭐ Wear rubber gloves when handling chilies.

⭐ Don't touch your eyes, mouth, or nose after handling chilies.

⭐ To cool your mouth, eat fatty dairy products like sour cream or ice cream.

> BEAN THERE, DONE THAT.

Sweet treats
Luckily, some Native American threw a tomahawk at a maple tree and discovered maple syrup. What would pancakes be without that!

Backfiring beans
In April 2012 a serving of nachos that weighed 4,689lb (2,127kg)—including 1,200lb (544kg) of beans—was dished up to athletes at the University of Kansas. You wouldn't want to be standing behind them later!

> AH, YOU'RE SO SWEET!

PEPPER SPRAY
·DOG/BEAR REPELLANT·
ON SALE HERE

Armed and dangerous
If a bear attacks, can you make him eat a chili? Maybe not, but you can spray him. The same chemical that makes chilies taste hot, is used in pepper spray.

WANT MORE?

WHO'S OSCAR?

Celebrities come and go, but the Academy Awards have their time in the limelight each year, and there's always one shining star that everyone wants to go home with—Oscar! This fancy figurine is fashioned after a knight grasping a sword and standing on top of a film reel. Anyone who's anyone in the motion-picture industry wants to get their mitts on this golden boy, but he only heads home with the best!

Oscar's official name is the "Academy Award of Merit."

OSCAR OVERLOAD

The Lord of the Rings: The Return of the King was nominated for 11 Academy Awards in 2003, and won all of them. It really was the Lord of the Awards!

UH-OH, I HOPE SHIRLEY DOESN'T DRESS ME UP IN A TU-TU!

WHERE ARE THE OTHER EIGHT?

Six of the best

In 1935, Shirley Temple was the first person to be presented with a Juvenile Award at the Oscars for her contribution to film. She was six years old!

Name of fame
The Oscar received its nickname in 1931. Rumor has it that when an Academy librarian first saw the statue, she said it looked like her Uncle Oscar. Thank goodness she didn't have an Uncle Percival!

GETTING PLATED IS QUITE A PRODUCTION!

Tread on the red
The red carpet is part of the show today, but why red? During the early days of rail travel, a crimson carpet at Grand Central Station led wealthy passengers to their train.

Vital statistics
The statuette is not quite 13.5in (35cm) tall and weighs 8.5lb (3.85kg). Made of a pewter-like alloy, it is covered in nickel silver and coated in 24-carat gold!

WANT MORE?

BANDITS AND BUST-UPS

During the 1800s, there were bandana bandits and bloody bust-ups at the drop of a 10-gallon hat in the wicked Wild West. Gunslinging gangs rustled horses and cattle, and outrageous outlaws like Billy the Kid got away with murder. Legend has it the Kid killed 21 men before he was gunned down—that would make one for each year of his life. But this boy fugitive was armed with charm as well as gunfire. He became a loved legend of the Wild West.

DON'T KID AROUND WITH THE KID!

A slippery start
Billy the Kid's first run-in with the law was over several pounds of butter that he stole from a rancher and sold. He got only a verbal licking for that.

BILLY THE KID

OFFICIAL NAME:
WILLIAM HENRY McCARTY

ALIASES:
WILLIAM H. BONNEY, HENRY ANTRIM, AND "THE KID"

OCCUPATION:
CRIMINAL

BORN:
NOVEMBER 23, 1859

ORPHANED: AGE 15

DIED:
JULY 14, 1881

CAUSE OF DEATH:
SHOT BY SHERIFF PAT GARRETT

Clean to mean
As a teen, the Kid was arrested over a bag of stolen laundry. He was locked up for a bit, but got real dirty after his release when he joined a gang of cold-blooded killers!

A handy trick

The Kid was of slight build and—surprise— he looked like a kid! He had small hands, but his wrists were wide. This was a sheriff's nightmare. It was easy for Billy to slip out of his handcuffs.

SHOOT, I REALLY DON'T WANT TO SHOOT!

More films have been made about Billy the Kid than any other outlaw.

Revolving revolvers

The Kid was a sure-fire show-off at twirling guns. He could take a revolver in each hand and twirl the guns in opposite directions at the same time.

SHOOT AND SPLIT

Many believe Billy the Kid was a good-hearted ruffian who got mixed up with the wrong crowd. But he became a hard core criminal with a death sentence on his head when he shot and killed a sheriff in 1880. The Kid escaped from jail by gunning down guards, jumping on a horse, and hoofing it out of town. The law finally caught up with him in 1881.

Sheriff Pat Garrett

WANT MORE?

Sheriff Pat Garrett brought Billy the Kid to justice at last ☆ www.thewildwest.org

THE WILD, WAY-OUT WEST

If you think frisbees are a modern invention, think again. During the 1800s children traveling west with their families along bumpy wagon trails took a play break now and then and flung disks of dry buffalo dung! With space in the canvas-covered wagons for food and supplies only, pioneer kids had left their books and toys behind. But who says dung can't be fun?

HOLD YOUR HORSES, I'M NOT DEAD YET!

Troubles on the trail
One in 10 pioneers died on the way west, but the wagons kept on rolling. A "watcher" would stay with the dying person, sometimes digging their grave in front of them. That's no sight for sore eyes!

LET ME GET RID OF THAT CIGARETTE. SMOKING'S BAD FOR YOU!

Annie Oakley

BUFFALO BILL'S AND
WILD WEST CONGRESS OF RO
RIDERS OF
WORLD.

RUFFLES AND RIFLES

Buffalo Bill Cody put on a circus of rough-riding antics and sharpshooting skills that made the Wild West world famous. One of his shooting stars was petticoat-clad Annie Oakley. Called "Little Sure Shot," this shy sharpshooter could shoot the ash off a cigarette while someone was smoking it!

Buffalo Bill

Chuck in your chips

Dung was not only useful for flinging. Pioneer children had regular chores and often pitched in to collect dried buffalo "chips" as fuel for fires.

Heading west across the plains

Draggin' a wagon

The west was windy as well as wild. One hopeful pioneer built a prototype Wind-Wagon with sails. It rollicked across the plains but then crashed!

WANT MORE?

More than half a million brave pioneers went west with wagons during the 1800s.

MAGIC OF DISNEY

Who would have thought that a little cartoon mouse could create all this fuss? Countless characters and innovative ideas whirled from the inventive mind of Walter Elias Disney, but Mickey Mouse was the one that made Walt a star. Disney is known as the "Father of Animation," but he could also be called the "father of imagination.'" Imagine that!

More than one million guests visited Disneyland in its first two months!

Dream with a theme

With so many lively characters, Walt must have needed a place to put them all! In 1955, he opened Disneyland, a theme park in Southern California. There are now 11 Disney theme parks. That's a lot of cups and saucers!

ARE YOU TAKING THE MICKEY OUT OF ME, LITTLE MOUSE?

I DON'T THINK THIS TEABAG IS BIG ENOUGH.

Walt made early
cartoons called
Laugh-O-Grams in
his backyard shed.

Mortimer Mouse?
Walt dreamed up Mickey Mouse on a train ride in 1928. The playful cartoon mouse escaped being named Mortimer by only a whisker. He can thank Mrs. Disney for giving him the moniker of Mickey!

Animation creation
In 1937, Disney's *Snow White and the Seven Dwarfs* became the first full-length animated film produced by a studio. Disney won a special Oscar, made with one large statuette and seven miniature ones. Hope he wasn't too Bashful to accept it!

Donald Duck's
middle name is
Fauntleroy. Mickey
Mouse doesn't have
a middle name.

CAN I BE PAID IN DOG BISCUITS, PLEASE?

Groomed for greatness
Disney made movies with human stars and animal actors, too. But even pups had to place their paw prints on the dotted line to secure their Hollywood contracts!

WANT MORE?

Walt Disney arrived in Hollywood with just 40 dollars!

INDEX

NOT-FOR-PARENTS
U.S.A.
EVERYTHING YOU EVER WANTED TO KNOW

1st Edition
Published September 2012

Conceived by Weldon Owen in partnership with Lonely Planet
Produced by Weldon Owen Publishing
Northburgh House, 10 Northburgh Street
London, EC1V 0AT, UK

weldonowenpublishing.com

Copyright © 2012 Weldon Owen Publishing

WELDONOWEN
PUBLISHING

WELDON OWEN LTD
Managing Director Sarah Odedina
Publisher Corinne Roberts
Creative Director Sue Burk
Sales Director Laurence Richard
Sales Manager, North America Ellen Towell
Project Editor Shan Wolody
Designer Adam Walker
Design Assistant Haylee Bruce
Index Puddingburn Publishing Services
Production Director Dominic Saraceno
Production Controller Tristan Hanks

Published by
Lonely Planet Publications Pty Ltd ABN 36 005 607 983
90 Maribyrnong St, Footscray, Victoria 3011, Australia

ISBN 978-1-7432-1423-7

Printed in China

A WELDON OWEN PRODUCTION

Credits and Acknowledgments

Key tl=top left; tcl=top center left; tc=top center; tcr=top center right;
tr=top right; cl=center left; c=center; cr=center right; bl=bottom left;
bcl=bottom center left; bc=bottom center; bcr=bottom center right;
br=bottom right; bg = background.

2br, 17tc, 20-21bc, 28bl, 28-29bc, 29br, cr, 32-33bg, 36-37cl, 41br, 48cl,
58-59c, 59br, 64cl, 79br, 88cr, 89cl, 90bl, br, 93cr, tc **Alamy;** 44-45c
Bridgeman Art Library; 2bc, 3br, 8-9bc, 9tl, tr, 10br, tr, 10-11bc, 11cl, cr,
13c, 14bl, cl, tr, 19br, c, 20bl, 21cr, tr, 22bl, 22-23tc, 23br, c, 24bl, tc, 25c, cl, cr,
tr, 26cl, 26-27bc, 27cl, 30tr, 30-31c, 31tcr, 40bc, 41cl, 42bl, 42-43c, 46tr,
48-49c, 50-51bc, 51c, 53tc, 54bc, tr, 55bl, 56cl, 56-57c, 57br, tc, 58bl, 60bc,
60-61bc, 61br, c, cl, tr, 62-63c, 63bc, tr, 64tl, 64-65c, 66-67tc, 68bc, 69tr,
70-71c, 74bc, tr, 75cr, tc, 76cl, 76-77bc, 77br, 78bl, tr, 78-79c, 79cr, 80bc, c,
81br, 82cl, 84-85c, 86bl, br, 89br, tr, 92bl, 92-93c, 93br **Corbis;** 3bc, 12tr, 13br
tl, 16c, 22cl, 24cr, tr, 33br, cr, 37tc, 42br, 43br, 52c, cl, 65cr, 72tr, 82tr, 88br,
90tcl, tcr, 91tr, 94tr **Dreamstime;** 12bc, tc, 16bl, 16-17c, 18cl, 26tr, 27br, 38c,
39cl, 47r, 72bc, 81cr, tl, 90-91c **Getty Images;** 45cr **Granger Collection;**
2bl, 3bl, 4c, 8bl, c, tr, 9bcr, br, c, tcr, 11br, 12tcr, 13bl, cl, tr, 14br, 15bg, bl, bc, c,
tr, 16c, l, 17br, r, 18tr, 18-19bg, 20cl, 22bc, br, 23bc, bl, 26bc, tr, 27bc, 28tr,
29tc, 30bc, bl, c, 31br, tr, 32c, 33bcr, tl, 34cl, 35bl, br, 36cl, 36-37tc, 37br, c,
38bcl, bl, tr, 39tl, tr, 40c, cr, tr, 42tc, 43bc, c, 44bc, bl, 46-47bl, 48b, tr, 49bl, br,
l, tc, 50bl, 50-51tc, 51br, tr, 52bc, tr, 53br, 55tc, tl, tr, 56bl, 56-57tc, 57c, l, 58c,
60cl, 61cr, 62bc, bl, br, c, tr, 64cr, 65cl, tc, tl, tl, 66bc, bcr, cl, 67bl, br, tr, 68c, tc,
tcr, tl, 69bc, tc, tcl, 70bl, br, tl, tr, 72cr, 73bc, br, c, cl, cr, tc, 74c, cl, 75cl, tl,
76tcr, 77bl, c, cr, tl, tr, 78-79bg, 79tl, 80br, 81cl, 83cr, tl, tl, 84bl, c, 85br, c, tr,
86-87bg, tc, 87bl, br, 88bcr, bl, c, cl, tcr, 89tc, tcl, 92br, c, 93tl, 94bc, bc, bc, bl,
br, tc, 95bc, bc, bl, br, br, tc, tc, tc, tcl, tl, tr **iStockphoto.com;** 21br, 22c, 29tl,
44cl, 70bg, 71bl, br, 85bc, 94bcr **Shutterstock;** 19tl **Smithsonian Air and
Space Museum;** 34br **Wikipedia.**

All frames and borders courtesy of **iStockphoto.com** except 16bl, 48-49c,
56cl, 69tc, 76cl, 82cl courtesy of **Shutterstock.**

All repeated image motifs courtesy of **iStockphoto.com.**

Illustrations

Cover illustrations by **Chris Corr.**

1bc, br, 4-5l, 6bl, tr, 6-7c, 94tcr **Chris Corr;** 90bc **Geri Ford/The Art Agency;**
3tr, 18-19c **MBA Studios;** 35tc, 82-83bc **Dave Smith/The Art Agency;**
38-39c, 39cr **Dave Tracey.**

45tr, 63tl adapted from maps by **Will Pringle.**

All illustrations and maps copyright 2012 Weldon Owen Publishing

LONELY PLANET OFFICES

Australia Head Office
Locked Bag 1, Footscray, Victoria 3011
Phone 03 8379 8000 Fax 03 8379 8111

USA
150 Linden St, Oakland, CA 94607
Phone 510 250 6400 Toll free 800 275 8555 Fax 510 893 8572

UK
Media Centre, 201 Wood Lane, London W12 7TQ
Phone 020 8433 1333 Fax 020 8702 0112

lonelyplanet.com/contact